TOWN UNDERGROUND

BY JONATHAN EMMETT
ILLUSTRATED BY MAURIZIO DE ANGELIS

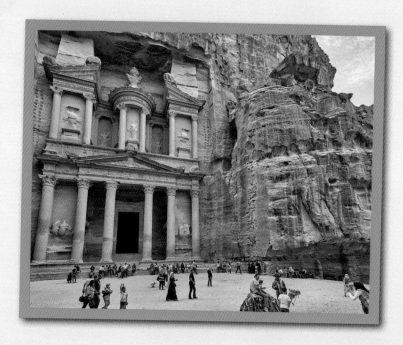

CONTENTS

CAMBRIDGE
UNIVERSITY PRESS

UCL
Institute of Education

LIVING UNDERGROUND

Many animals live underground.

Rabbits and foxes live in holes underground.

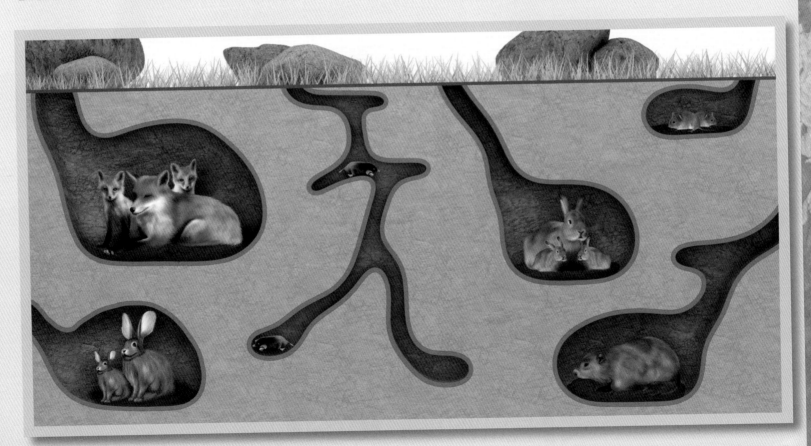

Bears and bats live in **caves**.

Caves are often underground.

3

Some people live in caves.

Some people live underground.

This is a village in Iran. The homes are in caves.

Some people dig their homes out of the ground.

Long ago, many people lived in this old underground town in Turkey. There was room for some animals, too. Nobody lives there now.

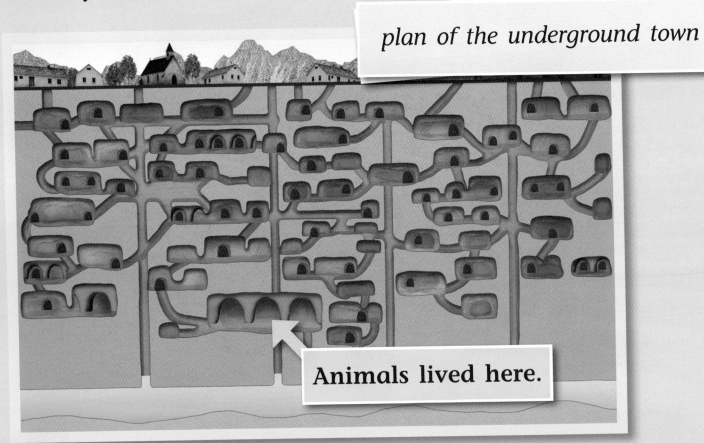

plan of the underground town

Animals lived here.

Today, **tourists** can visit the underground town.

MINING TOWNS

Some underground towns were in **mines**.
This town is in a salt mine in Poland.

This is how the salt mine looked when it was being used.

Tourists can now visit the mine.

This underground town is in an opal mine in Australia. People still live in the town. There are homes, shops, hotels and a restaurant.

An opal is a colourful jewel. Opals come from under the ground and are mined.

bookshop

shop

A pipe carries the opals out of the ground.

A machine digs out the opals.

This is how the mine looks above ground.

11

ROCK TEMPLES

Some of the oldest underground places were **temples** that were cut out of rock.

This is a temple in India.

This temple is in Jordan.

An Egyptian king called Rameses built this rock temple long ago so that people would remember him after he died.

inside the temple

15

SAFE AND SOUND

Sometimes people live underground to be safe. This tunnel leads to a town that has been dug inside a mountain.

the entrance to an underground town in America

Soldiers work in this underground office.

The town was built for the army to use in case there was a war.

SECRET HIDEAWAYS

Caves and underground spaces are good places to hide things. Here are some secret underground places from films and television shows.

Thunderbird 2's **hangar**

Batman's Batcave

SPECTRE's volcano rocket base from James Bond

UNDERGROUND HOUSES

People are still building underground homes because they want to live somewhere unusual. Here are two new homes which have been dug out of hillsides.

Malator House in Wales

Villa Vals in Switzerland

GLOSSARY

caves: large holes in hills or mountains

hangar: place to put airplanes

mines: places where something useful is dug out of the ground

temples: places where people can go to pray

tourists: people who visit a place for pleasure

INDEX

TOWN UNDERGROUND JONATHAN EMMETT

Teaching notes written by Sue Bodman and Glen Franklin

Using this book

Developing reading comprehension

This non-fiction report presents some ways of living and working underground. Photographs provide a view of the many ways to live and work underground. The non-fiction layout gives lots of opportunities to check information in the text with illustrations, and comment on the text meaning.

Grammar and sentence structure

- Sentence structures are more formal and complex (for example, *'Some of the oldest underground places were temples that were cut out of rock.'* on page 12).
- Some sentences demonstrate causality (such as: *'so that people would remember him after he died.'* on page 14; *'in case there was a war'* on page 17).

Word meaning and spelling

- Unfamiliar terms and vocabulary specific to the topic (*'entrance'*, *'mined'*, *'caves'*).
- Longer words require breaking into syllables (*'underground'*, *'Rameses'*, *'unusual'*).

Curriculum links

Geography – Children could develop mapping skills by drawing a plan of a home underground. This could be based on a home in the text, or a home they would like to live in.

Science and Nature – In this text, we see some animals that make their homes underground. They all have different reasons for doing so. Children could use the internet to explore why the animals named in the text – rabbits, foxes, bears and bats – choose to make their homes underground. Can they find any other animals that create burrows underground, or live in caves?

Learning Outcomes

Children can:

- use a variety of non-fiction page layouts
- problem-solve longer words by breaking them apart using familiar syllables
- consider events and provide reasons for why they might have happened.

A guided reading lesson

Book Introduction

Activate children's prior knowledge of the topic by asking them to explain what is meant by *'underground'*. Give each child a copy of the book. Read the title and the blurb with them. Ascertain that this is a non-fiction text and point out the range of features that the children will need to use – labels, captions, contents pages.

Orientation

Give a brief overview of the book:

This book will shows us many different types of underground homes. Some were lived in a long time ago. Some are still lived in.

Preparation

Page 2: This page deals with some animals that choose to live underground. The pictures show simple homes. The cross-section and the detail of the bats hanging upside down may require some explanation. The distinction between *'underground'* and *'cave'* is brought out. Say: *Tell me about the underground picture. What do you notice?* Repeat for the term *'cave'*. Discuss how some underground homes may be deep underground, some may be near the surface. Ask the children to predict how the 'towns' or human homes underground may differ to the animal homes pictured here.